THE PROFITABLE LAUNCH BLUEPRINT

The Ultimate Step-by-Step Guide to Doubling Your Profits

RONNIE TYLER

PROFITABLE LAUNCH BLUEPRINT
Copyright © 2021 Tyler New Media, LLC

All rights reserved.

No part of this publication may be reproduced, distributed, or transmitted in any form or by any means, including photocopying, recording, or other electronic or mechanical methods, without the prior written permission of the publisher, except in the case of brief quotations embodied in critical reviews and certain other noncommercial uses permitted by copyright law.

Printed in the United States of America

ISBN: 978-1-7350317-3-6

Special thanks to Master Author Coach Candice L. Davis for helping me write this book.

Book cover design and interior formatting by:
JERA Publishing

*Dedicated to my husband, Lamar.
Your passion for helping our community is so big
and your vision is unmatched.
I consider it an honor to be on this journey with you.*

Contents

Welcome to the Profitable Launch Blueprint 1

1. Why Launches Fail 11
2. 3 Ways to Double Your Launch Profits............... 23
3. The 4 Pillars of a Profitable Launch 31
4. The Profitable Launch Blueprint 51
5. How to Build a Launch Plan....................... 87
6. The Quick Launch 103
7. Getting Started with Your Profitable Launch 111

The Profitable Launch Blueprint Glossary............... 115

Welcome to the Profitable Launch Blueprint

I f you own a business and you want to dramatically increase your profits, you can. If you want to start a profitable business and quit your day job, you can make that happen. I say these things as someone who never imagined I'd become an entrepreneur. Some people are born with a desire to run their own business. They open their first lemonade stand in second grade and never look back. Not me. I took a much more conventional career path before I married into entrepreneurship.

After obtaining a math degree from Spelman College and a master's degree in electrical engineering from The Penn State University, I went to work for IBM as a certified project manager. I stayed there for seventeen years, and during that time, I managed expansive, complex software development projects with global teams in Australia, the UK, China, India, and Brazil. Our project budgets ran upwards of $30 million and returned much more in profits—though the only part of that profit I saw was my salary.

My husband, Lamar, on the other hand, was a career entrepreneur when I met him, but when we married, he took a full-time job in an effort to make me feel secure. Back then, I naively believed the risks of running your own business outweighed any potential benefits. It was important to me that our family maintain the consistency and stability of regular paychecks and corporate benefits, and I stayed on that path for many years.

I spent nearly two decades helping my employer earn many millions of dollars in profits. However, since I made the leap from corporate America to entrepreneurship, I've used those same skills to earn millions of dollars in profits in the businesses I co-own with my husband. Instead of pouring my talents and hard work into someone else's business, I'm creating a legacy for my family. I also coach other entrepreneurs to run their businesses more profitably so they can build wealth for themselves and create the kind of financial freedom that's nearly impossible to attain while working for someone else.

Because of our success, I've appeared on national news outlets, like CNBC, NBC's *Today* show, and NPR, and in national magazines, including *Parenting*, *Essence*, and *Entrepreneur*. I've won awards, like the Ebony Power 100 and the Atlanta Voice 50 under

50, and taken the stage to share with thousands of people—at events like Blogging While Brown, ICON (Infusionsoft's small business conference) and our own TSP Live and TSP Game Plan—a little of what I've learned as I've launched and scaled two businesses, Black and Married with Kids and Traffic Sales & Profit, with my husband. Each of these opportunities has given me a chance to tell my story and, hopefully, inspire other entrepreneurs. None of this would've happened if I hadn't left the "security" of my corporate position.

In 2007, three years into our marriage, my husband and I started the blog that would grow into Tyler New Media while both keeping our day jobs. Black and Married with Kids publishes content focused on uplifting and encouraging marriages and families in the African American community. With the blog, we pushed the envelope, stretched ourselves, and up-leveled our standards every year, and our blog grew into a movement. We hired editors and a staff of up to forty writers, and we grew an international platform from our website, blackandmarriedwithkids.com.

Over that time, we built a huge audience, and we learned a lot about online marketing and sales. We soon realized we could serve our audience in deeper ways by creating products and services designed with their unique needs and wants in mind. We produced films and orchestrated multi-city movie tours, created online courses, and published ebooks and audiobooks.

Our blog became a full-fledged business. (To find out more about how we built our first brand, check out Lamar's book, *The Gatekeepers Are Gone* on Amazon.)

In 2010, Lamar left his job to work in the business full time. I, on the other hand, held on to my position with IBM, but by 2013, when the company was going through layoffs, my heart wasn't really in the job anymore. Even though I was a top performer, I was going through the motions every day. I wanted out, but instead of quitting, I decided to hold on until I could get a severance package in one of the layoff rounds.

During this time, I worked my full-time job while raising four children with my husband, managing the writers at Black and Married with Kids, and running our marketing campaigns. I had a lot on my plate, and all the juggling sometimes made me feel like I was stealing time from my employer or shortchanging my family. I worked nights and weekends, trying to get it all done, but I never felt like I was giving my best to my job, my business, or my family. But I still didn't quit IBM.

One day, I settled down to work at home, pleased with myself for having gotten my two middle children off for the first day of school. We'd even taken their "first day" pictures to share with family and friends and memorialize the moment. My oldest was in college, and the youngest, Jodi, was home with me until her preschool started classes the following week. Everything was as it should be. At least, I thought it was.

A few hours into the day, my phone rang. When I answered, my daughter's preschool teacher asked, "Why isn't Jodi in school today?" My daughter had missed the first day of school and all the fun and excitement of starting off the new year with her classmates. In the process of trying to manage my job, our business, and the kids' schedules, all at the same time, I had somehow mixed up the dates. Something had to give. I realized it was time to say goodbye to the career I'd spent almost two decades building.

When I finally told my manager about my decision to leave IBM, he was relieved. He had the difficult task of laying off people who really wanted to keep their jobs, and he didn't enjoy it. It was so much easier for him to let me go because I actually wanted to leave. He explained that, based on my performance, he'd never considered laying me off, but he agreed to include me in the next round of layoffs. A few months later, I was working in the business full time. Ironically, the money I received with the layoff—money I'd held out for over several months when I could have been investing my time and talents in our business—didn't last me very long at all.

As our brand's reach expanded, other entrepreneurs and would-be entrepreneurs wanted to know how we built our business. They wanted to know how we consistently grew and engaged with our audience. They wanted to know how we both managed to leave our corporate jobs and focus on full-time entrepreneurship together. Recognizing a clear need for someone to provide this information for our audience, we started our second brand, Traffic Sales & Profit. Through TSP, we offer coaching, consulting, and training for entrepreneurs. We teach them to drive more traffic, convert more leads to sales, and make more profits in their businesses.

Today, Traffic Sales & Profit is the go-to platform for African American entrepreneurs who want to build a thriving business. In addition to coaching and training, we offer a twelve-month business mastermind group, which has helped hundreds of business owners reach their first six figures. We've also seen several entrepreneurs hit seven figures while participating in the mastermind and implementing what they learned from us. These business owners don't just absorb the strategies and tactics we share. They take action on them.

Through the TSP Mastermind, I've coached hundreds of entrepreneurs to develop their project management skills and successfully launch their products and services. Teaching entrepreneurs to increase profits in their online businesses has been some of the most rewarding work I've ever had the pleasure to do. That positive impact ripples beyond one entrepreneur and one business to create prosperity for their employees and vendors and for their family and community.

In the process of building our two brands, we've had several successful six-figure and seven-figure launches. I've learned a lot from what we did well—and what went wrong—in every launch. In my work with entrepreneurs, some commonalities among them have also become obvious to me. Most importantly, I realized every business owner is a project manager for their business, whether they want to be or not. It doesn't matter if you self-identify as a project manager or don't even know what a project manager does. Until you can hire someone to help you manage your launches and other projects, you are the project manager for your business. The good news is that, with the steps in *The Profitable Launch Blueprint*, you can do that job well.

You Are a Project Manager

A project manager's responsibilities include planning the project—including budget and timeline—organizing and directing the completion of the project, and guiding and executing the completion of the project. A project manager owns the success or failure of the project. If you're a solopreneur, micropreneur, or small business owner, and you don't have a team member dedicated to managing projects, you are the de facto project manager for your business.

The obvious problem with this is that most business owners have received little or no training on how to plan and manage projects. This lack of exposure to project management best practices is at the core of most of the challenges and frustrations entrepreneurs experience. Never is this more obvious than when they launch a product or service. Too often, their launches miss the mark. Too often, the launches are less than profitable. Usually, these shortfalls aren't because of a lack of effort. These owners simply don't know where to begin to create a solid launch plan and execute it effectively. My goal, for more than a decade now, has been to help my fellow entrepreneurs get past those challenges, learn what they need to know, and enjoy one profitable launch after another.

My project management experience has been the secret weapon we've used to build our business. It's the foundation for the six-figure and seven-figure launches we've enjoyed. We've used the knowledge and skills I developed as a certified project manager to strategically plan every element of our launches and properly execute on them. Now, it's my mission to bring these same principles to business owners like you so you can have more success with your launches and the overall health and profitability of your business.

Launching is simply the process of releasing a new product or service to your market. Particularly in the online business world, where courses, programs, and products may not be evergreen and may only be available within a limited time frame, launching can also apply to products and services you release again and again. Profitable launches can change the trajectory of your business and take it from struggling to surviving and from surviving to thriving. Wherever your business is now, learning to launch efficiently and successfully can take it to the next level.

The Profitable Launch Blueprint consists of five steps:
1. Plan
2. Prep
3. Promote
4. Launch
5. Wrap up

This blueprint works. It works if you're launching a product or a service. It works if you're launching a low-price offer or a premium offer. It works if you've launched a hundred times before or you're just dipping your toe into the waters of entrepreneurship with your first launch. The Profitable Launch Blueprint works for full-time entrepreneurs and side hustlers alike. Launching without a proven system is like trying to bake a cake from scratch without a recipe. You probably won't like your result. But when you have a system like this in place and follow it, there's no limit to the goals you can achieve or the money you can make.

(**Note:** I use "product" throughout the rest of this book to refer to any product or service you're selling because the same process applies. Yes, service providers, these strategies will work for you too. It doesn't matter if you're selling physical products, digital products, group services, or one-on-one services. You need a plan.)

CHAPTER ONE

Why Launches Fail

Here's the truth many business coaches don't want you to know: *Some launches will fail.*

After weeks or months spent creating your product and several more weeks doing all the things you thought you were supposed to do to get ready to launch, the day finally arrives. You open cart. Maybe you send one more email to your list or post on social media to let your followers know it's time to buy. You pour a cup of coffee and sit down to watch the money roll in from new clients. At first, there's no action, so you keep clicking the refresh button, hoping to see the numbers go up or a "You've got a sale!" email come in. But you're wasting your time. The numbers don't move. No one is buying. Over the next couple of days, a few sales trickle in, but nowhere near the volume you expected. Your launch has failed.

The gurus make it look easy. If you follow influencers who share their huge launch numbers, you might start to believe you can copy their launch and create the same results. It's natural to think so. You get all their emails. You click on their social media ads, sign up for their webinars, and take notes on how they present their offer. In theory, you should be able to replicate their success.

In truth, however, you probably see less than ten percent of what it took for them to create those seemingly effortless launches with the huge pay days. You have no idea how big their budget was, how many ads they ran, how large or how engaged their email list was, how many affiliates promoted the launch, or what kind of team they had to help them plan, prep, promote, launch, and wrap up. Trying to copy their process, when most of it happens behind the scenes, is a gamble you're likely to lose.

A failed launch can literally knock the wind out of you as you sit there, wondering what went wrong and how you can make it right. If this has ever happened to you, you're not alone. Most entrepreneurs who've been in business for a while know the pain of a failed launch. I've had a few of my own, and each one was a devastating blow. It took days to rebound from missing the goals we'd set.

Keep in mind that launch goals aren't necessarily based on profits or revenue. Sometimes, the desired end result is more leads, followers, or exposure. Whatever your goal is, if you don't achieve it, the negative impact can be very real. Besides a lack of profit or visibility, a failed launch can cause you to lose confidence in your product or in yourself. It can cause you to abandon a perfectly good product or even give up on entrepreneurship altogether.

In most cases, the problem isn't your product. You're an expert in your field. You spent years developing your knowledge and expertise before you ever sat down to create the product. If you're like most of the ambitious entrepreneurs I meet, you're committed to producing quality. The problem isn't you either. It's not that people don't like you or what you represent. A host of reasons may contribute to not reaching your desired launch results, but they have nothing to do with you as a person or your product.

Here are the five common reasons launches fail:
1. Wrong offer
2. Lack of visibility
3. Wrong launch strategy or no launch strategy
4. Lack of planning
5. Fear

Make or Break Your Launch with Your Offer

Your offer includes your price and how you present your product to your target audience. If your price isn't right or the way you position your product doesn't resonate with your audience, they won't purchase. Fortunately, you have several ways you can adjust your offer to connect with your audience.

Perhaps you need to raise or lower the price. If it isn't comparable to the price of comparable products and services in the marketplace, and you may confuse your audience. Underpricing can cause buyers to question the value of your product or service, and overpricing can send them running to look for a better deal. Your price may be right, but your audience may not be ready to pay in full or may not want to use the one payment processor you've chosen. A lack of payment options can stop potential customers from clicking the buy button.

It may be that you failed to demonstrate why the price is appropriate by establishing trust and communicating the benefits of your product. You may need to offer more social proof, demonstrating to your audience that people like them or experts they admire believe in your product. Perhaps you need to bundle your product with other products or include bonuses to increase the perception of the value of your offer. Whatever strategies you employ, you have to demonstrate the benefits and value of your offer. If you didn't get the launch results you wanted, look at the variables of your offer and determine which you'll change for your next launch.

Make or Break Your Launch with Visibility

Sometimes, a launch fails simply because no one knows about it. If you have no audience when you open cart, you're launching in a vacuum. People can't buy what they don't know about, and they're unlikely to buy from you before they get to know, like, and trust you. That requires you to build and nurture an audience.

You may have a great product at the right price, but if you don't get enough eyes on it, your launch will fail. Consistently building your audience, including your email list, SMS contacts, and social media following, will help you avoid this common cause of launch failures. You also have the option to borrow someone else's audience by offering influencers the opportunity to promote your products as affiliates. Your affiliates win by receiving a commission on referred sales, and you win by reaching a new audience, but build those affiliate relationships before you need them.

Make or Break Your Launch with Strategy

There's no shortage of ways you can launch your product. You can use any combination of webinars, master classes, email campaigns, paid ads, challenges, and other methods. However, if the strategy you select doesn't work for your offer, your product, or your audience, then your launch will fail. Fortunately, you can follow some simple rules to choose an effective launch strategy.

If you're launching a low-ticket offer, you can likely use a launch strategy that involves less education and less personal touch for your audience. For instance, if you're selling a T-shirt for $27 or a digital course for less than $100, you won't need to commit as much time, energy, or money to educating your audience or training them to understand your product. In that case, your strategy may be as simple as getting some ads out on social media and linking to your sales page, where people can purchase. For lower-ticket offers, your potential customers typically won't need a lot of explanation from you, and because the price is low, more people will be willing to buy, on the spot, when they first visit your sales page.

For a mid-priced product, you probably need to provide more education to your audience and take a high-touch approach by communicating more about the product. If your product is priced from about $1,000 up to about $3,500, then you might want to present a webinar to educate your audience about the benefits of the product and why it can work for them before you offer them the chance to buy. You might go live on social media to answer questions or present an all-day virtual summit to create value and educate your audience so they understand the results they can get with your product.

As your price increases, the level of training and personal connection you provide your prospective customers typically needs to increase at the same rate. For a product that costs $10,000 or $15,000, prospects will likely need more education and training and more connection with you. This could be a live event, where you establish yourself as the expert by sharing your expertise and providing case studies, testimonials, and proof of concept over two or three days. The increased communication will allow you to draw in your potential customers and launch and sell your product to people who understand the value and are ready to buy. In that case, a five-figure sticker price won't come as a shock to them, and a percentage of your audience will be happy to pay it because they'll expect your product to be worth it.

Your launch strategy matters. It can make a huge difference in whether you hit your sales goals or fall short. Because strategy is so critical, every entrepreneur should expect to test different methods to see what works for your product and your audience.

Make or Break Your Launch with Planning

Much of this book focuses on planning for your launch because a solid plan sets you up for success with the whole process of launching, from beginning to end. Most people have heard the saying that failing to plan is planning to fail, but they still don't plan properly for their launches. It's not because they don't want to do it. A failure to plan is the biggest reason launches fail. Most people simply have no idea how to effectively plan. With the Profitable Launch Blueprint, you should never have that problem again.

Keep in mind that planning well requires taking into account that your launch doesn't end when you stop promoting and close cart. You still need to get through a very important step. Entrepreneurs, especially those who fail to adequately plan, often get to this wrap-up stage and discover they're too exhausted to do it right. If you plan for your wrap-up, however, you'll end your launch on a high note. You'll have assets to reuse and data to analyze and learn from, and your customers will be much happier with their purchases. (We'll dive more deeply into wrap-up and the other the parts of a plan in chapter four.)

Creating a launch plan allows you to understand all the work, time, effort, and financial investment your launch will require from beginning to end. Planning makes it possible for you to consider potential problems that could arise in any phase of your launch and deal with them proactively. You can't wing a successful launch, but you can absolutely plan for one.

Make or Break Your Launch with Mindset

Finally, one of the biggest reasons your launch fails is you. But the good news is *you can change you*. If you don't know how to launch effectively, you've already started on your way to resolving your lack of knowledge by picking up this book. Implement what you learn here, and you'll see a huge improvement in your launches. You can always overcome a lack of knowledge by investing in education and training and applying what you learn. Launching successfully isn't a skill reserved for a few special people. You can learn everything necessary to create your own profitable launches. Hone your skills by launching again and again, and learn from what goes well and what doesn't.

An even bigger issue than lack of knowledge, when it comes to launch failures, is fear. Fear causes you to play small. Fear causes you to second-guess yourself, to lose confidence in your abilities as an expert or in the quality of your product. Fear causes you to self-sabotage. Maybe you're scared because you launched in the past and failed. You don't put in the needed effort for future launches because you really don't believe you can succeed. You don't take the action you know you should because you're afraid to fail again. Or you've never launched at all, but you're afraid to go big your first time out because, if you fail, you think the result will be public embarrassment.

Fear can rob you of the discipline you need to do the work required to have a successful launch. Even when you know what to do, you may resist investing the time, effort, and money you know you should invest. After all, if you only do the launch halfway, and it doesn't succeed, you can always tell yourself it failed because you didn't really try. If you play full out and it doesn't work, you'll face a bigger challenge of identifying what went wrong, and you may worry there's something inherently wrong with you or your product. It can be easier to not really try at all.

Some people like to say there are no failures, only opportunities. I disagree. From my experience both failure and opportunity are part of an entrepreneur's reality. Let's be real. If you spend six months launching your product and you don't get any sales, that's a failure. If you invest $100,000 in marketing for your launch, and you only make $20,000, that's a failure. Failures happen.

When you experience failure, realize it can also present an opportunity if you approach it the right way. You have the chance to learn why your launch failed. You can improve your offer, your visibility, your strategy, your plan, and how you manage fear. Accept failure as a possibility and work on your mindset to move forward anyway. The right mindset is essential to this process. Believe success is possible for you. Be willing to learn. Understand failure isn't the end of the road.

If you've had a failed launch, use what you learn here to analyze it, optimize it, and then launch again. The Profitable Launch Blueprint can transform your launches from failures to huge, profitable successes. My years of experience as a project manager, as an entrepreneur managing my own launches, and coaching and teaching other entrepreneurs led me to create this system to make it easier for entrepreneurs to launch successfully. Follow this process, and discover what it can do for you and your bottom line.

> Visit profitablelaunchblueprint.com/resources to download free tools and templates to support your next profitable launch.

CHAPTER TWO

3 Ways to Double Your Launch Profits

What if I told you that you could double or even triple your launch profits this year? And what if I told you that you could do it with your existing products, without creating anything new, even if you only have one product? If you've had semi-successful launches in the past, there are always opportunities to improve. These simple changes can result in significant increases in profit. While there are no guarantees, there are some commonly overlooked ways to increase your launch profits.

Three ways to double your launch profits:
1. More marketing
2. More follow-up
3. More launches

More Marketing

Adding more marketing to your launch plan is a no-brainer. It stands to reason that, if you get your offer in front of more of the right people, you'll have more potential leads, more potential customers, and more potential conversions from prospects to sales. Most entrepreneurs fail to get their products in front of enough people. They just don't do enough marketing, but with proper planning and preparation for your launch, you can increase your paid and organic promotional efforts to get more eyes on your offer. For a variety of reasons, not the least of which is fear, many entrepreneurs hesitate to increase their marketing efforts. But more marketing is one of the best ways to reach your launch goals.

Early on, we embraced the use of more marketing to increase our launch profits. For example, we typically promote our webinars for two to four weeks. In a two-week promotional period, we send ten to fourteen emails to push people to register for the webinar. Then, we send eight to ten emails to push registrants to attend. (This may seem like a lot of emails to your list. But many of the emails simply provide relevant content and a link to the webinar. All the emails aren't hard pushes.) After we host the live webinar, we'll typically send another two to four emails to encourage registrants to watch the replay, and those emails go to all registrants whether they attended live or not. Finally, we send four to six more emails to encourage people to purchase the product we offered during the webinar.

All total, we send as many as thirty-two emails to promote the webinar and the product the webinar sells. In conjunction with the emails, we promote on Twitter, Facebook, and Instagram, the social media platforms which have proven most effective for our brand. This includes going live on Facebook or Instagram to generate buzz. We don't hold back on our marketing efforts because we've found more marketing equals more sales.

On top of email marketing and organic social media marketing, we also run paid Facebook ads to encourage people to register for the webinar. Facebook ads are a huge and ever-changing topic, and I could easily go down a rabbit hole trying to explain how and why Facebook ads. Your ad strategy will depend on too many variables to parse here, but I can tell you how we approach ads.

We include Facebook ads in the marketing for every launch we do, and we endeavor to take full advantage of Facebook's ad system. We target our ideal customers to entice them to register for our webinars. We also use ads to retarget people who click on an ad but don't register. These follow-up ads give them more reasons to register. Investing money in Facebook ads—with a clear targeting strategy—has made a huge difference in our profits and in the profits our clients enjoy once they start to employ similar strategies. We've found it's worth the investment to work with a knowledgeable professional who can help you design and run your ads.

Marketing can only improve your launches when you adequately plan and prepare. Most entrepreneurs have every intention of using all these promotional tools for their launches. Unfortunately, once the launch begins, they're only able to do a fraction of those marketing activities because they're trying to do it all in the spur of the moment. The launch is underway, and they're struggling to create ad content or social media posts. Most people only do a small percentage of the marketing they intend to do because they become overwhelmed by everything going on during the launch period. With proper planning and preparation, you can get it all done.

More Follow-up

You can also increase your launch profits this year with more follow-up. Businesses lose so much money because they fail to follow up with potential customers. Take the example of a free live webinar we host to launch a product. We've found we can increase our sales by twenty to forty and sometimes even fifty percent, by continuing to follow up with the people who attended and those who didn't attend, every day until our launch period ends. Every day, there are things we can do to follow up, and sometimes that even includes hosting another webinar or two or three.

Using technology, you also have an opportunity to follow up by using an abandoned cart sequence. If someone comes to your sales page and sees your offer, but they don't purchase, then there are ways you can follow up using automated systems. You can retarget people who landed on your sales page via Facebook advertisements. If they started to purchase but didn't complete the process, you may be able to follow-up with emails. If you have their phone numbers, you can also take the old-fashioned approach and pick up the phone. Ask why they didn't buy, and to try to convince them to purchase. Finally, if sales or consultation calls are part of your sales process, then you need to follow up with your leads at least eight to twelve times to ensure you've done an adequate job of pitching your product.

If you want to increase your revenue during your launches, look for opportunities to follow up more. At the same time remember that, to do more follow-up, you have to plan properly. You have to create a system to ensure the follow-up happens every time it should.

More Launches

I often have the same conversation with entrepreneurs. Here's how it goes.

Entrepreneur: I'm launching my book/product/service. I'm going to have a huge launch and start selling it in January.

Me: That's great! I can't wait to see it!

6 Months Later

Me: How'd your launch go? How are your sales?

Entrepreneur: Oh, I haven't launched yet.

3 Months Later

Entrepreneur: I finally launched!

Me: That's great! How'd it go?

Entrepreneur: Oh, it went okay. But I don't think people are really interested in that kind of book/product/service right now.

In that all-too-common scenario, the entrepreneur has let most of the year pass by without a product launch. If they had launched in January, when they said they wanted to launch, they could have done several launches over that period and increased profits by launching more. That doesn't have to be your experience. You can launch more often with thorough planning and disciplined execution of the plan.

That's the whole purpose of the Profitable Launch Blueprint. It's designed to make you more effective with your planning so you can make the most of every launch. Not only will your launches be more profitable, but with the skills you develop along the way, you can streamline your launch process and effectively and efficiently carry out more launches throughout the year.

> Visit profitablelaunchblueprint.com/resources to download free tools and templates to support your next profitable launch.

CHAPTER THREE

The 4 Pillars of a Profitable Launch

Before we dive into the Profitable Launch Blueprint, there are a few critical foundational components you need to be aware of and make sure you have in place. They're critical not only to the success of any launch but also to running your business, so give them the necessary time and attention before, during, after launching your product.

These are the four pillars of a profitable launch:

List

Your list, made up of your followers and subscribers, is the first component of your profitable launch. Ideally, you'll start building your list long before your launch begins and continually build it regardless of whether you're planning to launch soon or not. Subscribers and followers have slightly different relationships with your business, but both are valuable.

Subscribers are members of lists you own, including email lists, SMS lists, phone lists, and customer lists. You aren't beholden to any particular platform to reach these subscribers because they've given you their direct contact information and permission to communicate with them. Subscribers are a warm audience. They've already demonstrated they want something from you and trust you enough to give you their contact information. They may even have bought something from you in the past. Typically, these subscribers have joined your list in exchange for a lead magnet, a free offer from you in exchange for their contact information. This could be anything from a simple checklist to an ebook, print book, or webinar, or some of your time in a free consultation call.

Your followers may or may not be as warm as your subscribers, but they're still a warm audience. They've shown an interest in your brand, your content, and what you have to offer. They've connected with you by subscribing to your podcast or YouTube channel, following you on Instagram or Facebook, or connecting with you on LinkedIn or other platforms. Your followers may be members of your social media groups or have chatted with you via messenger bots. Followers are engaged with you in some way; however, unless they give you their contact information, you can only reach followers through the platform where they've chosen to follow you. If the platform went away or made sweeping changes, you might lose those relationships.

You don't own the contact information for your followers, but that doesn't mean you shouldn't cultivate a following. Popular social media platforms aren't likely to go away any time soon, and they provide unique opportunities for your business. These platforms allow you to engage with your followers, get feedback from them, communicate with them in real time, livestream video to them, and more. In addition, growing your following on some of these social media platforms will make running paid ads much more effective when you get to the promotions phase of your launch.

Growing your number of subscribers and followers should be an ongoing activity for all entrepreneurs because, as discussed in Chapter One, one of the biggest challenges entrepreneurs face is launching to no one. Let's face it. Your launch only works if you get your offer in front of enough people. Even if your products don't require a lot of education before customers buy, you may need to spend time building trust before you can sell. You can accomplish that by building your list of subscribers and followers and consistently communicating with them.

Too many entrepreneurs don't even think about their list until they're planning a launch. They spend months, or even a year or two, building their product or designing their service, never once asking, "Who am I actually going to sell this to once I'm ready to launch?" Don't make that mistake. Build your list along the way. If you keep them engaged, some of those people will be waiting for you to make an offer.

You can also get input and feedback from your subscribers and followers by asking about their biggest challenges and sharing your ideas for products you're considering creating. The input they provide will help you develop a product that appeals to them, understand how to design your offer, and prepare for any objections you need to overcome in your promotions.

> Visit profitablelaunchblueprint.com/resources to download the free "Biggest Challenge" email template to easily get the feedback you need.

Finally, your list is also essential to maximizing paid ads for your launch promotions. When you have an existing audience to launch to, your paid advertising is less expensive because you can target custom audiences, made up your subscribers and followers, and look-alike audiences, made up of people with psychographics and demographics similar to your email subscribers. When you already have a list, you can build buzz weeks and even months ahead of your launch. You can take your subscribers on a journey as you develop your product and create anticipation.

There are so many advantages to building your email list and real disadvantages to avoiding this process. To learn more about lead magnets, list-building, and growing your audience, check out the step-by-step system in *Traffic, Sales & Profit*, by Lamar Tyler, at freetspbook.com.

Technology

Technology plays a significant role in the level of success you achieve in your launch. These software programs and apps make it easier to do business at any time, and it's wise to have them in place before you attempt to launch. These tools facilitate everything from communication with your team and with your audience to order processing and fulfillment. Launching without them just doesn't make sense.

The technology you use for your launch may include the following:
- Project management software
- Collaboration software

- Landing pages and sales pages
- Email marketing services and/or customer relationship management software
- E-commerce and payment processors
- Online meeting and webinar platforms
- Membership platforms

Each of these tools has a specific purpose. Project management tools help you in the organization and planning of your launch. Collaboration tools, like Google Suite, provide an efficient way to communicate across your team and with vendors and a place to organize and store documents and other files. You can also use the chat feature for collaboration. Landing pages and sales pages are standalone webpages where you can lead prospects to sign up for your email list, register for webinars, buy your products, and more. Email marketing software or your customer relationship management software helps you organize customer contact information and communicate with customers via email. This is the software you'll use to send out your email campaign for your launch.

Your e-commerce or credit card payment software, such as Shopify or Stripe, will allow you to receive payments, usually for a small fee per transaction. Online meeting or webinar platforms, like Zoom, Skype, or GoToMeeting are necessary if a webinar is a part of your launch plan. A membership platform gives you a place to house online products and services, like courses, videos, and downloads, and control who can access that content. Your specific launch plan will determine what technology you need, but these are all examples of the technology your launch might require.

If your technology fails, it can negatively impact your launch in a huge way. There's no worse feeling than kicking off your launch and investing so much time, energy, and money, only to find out you're losing sales because your website or landing page is down, your orders aren't processing, or you lost connectivity during your webinar, right at the moment you started your sales pitch. No technology runs perfectly, but when you have a launch plan in place, you create time to test your technology and make sure it runs as smoothly as possible. When you follow your plan, you'll also have the time and energy to monitor your technology and fix anything broken in your process as quickly as possible.

These tools can make launching much easier, but a lack of technology should never prevent you from launching. If you don't have the budget or the technical know-how for some of these tools, you can still find ways to launch your product. I've seen entrepreneurs pull off very successful, very profitable launches with printed sales sheets and credit card processing forms. I've seen others launch with nothing more than a PayPal link. A lack of technical expertise or limited access to technology should never be an excuse for you to push off your launch or never launch at all.

Instead, make it your goal to improve your technology with every launch. If your first launch revolves around a simple sales page, then for your next launch you can improve upon the copy and the graphics on that page. You can add an upsell offer or a downsell offer to your initial sales page, using slightly more sophisticated technology. Each time you launch, look at opportunities to improve how you use technology.

Technology is constantly changing, and my choice of software for each of these areas is always what works best at any given time.

> To download a list of my current technology recommendations, visit profitablelaunchblueprint.com/resources.

Irresistible Offer

The next pillar in a profitable launch is your offer. No matter how great your product is, it won't sell if you don't have a great offer. As it pertains to launching, the price of your product isn't the only factor that makes a great offer. There are a few other things you need to consider before you get into developing your offer.

First, honestly assess your product. Ask yourself the following questions:
1. Is this a high-quality product I can confidently stand behind?
2. Is it worth my time and money to launch this product?
3. Is my product priced correctly for my audience and as compared to similar products?

If you can answer yes to all those questions, then you have a product worth offering. However, if you're unsure, about the answer to any of those questions, get a second opinion from your business coach or mastermind group. Don't create your offer until you can answer each of those questions in the affirmative.

Next, assess your traffic sources. Do you have the ability to generate traffic that will get your offer seen? Remember your offer only works if you can get it in front of enough of the right people. Get clear about all your potential traffic sources, starting with your email list. Look at your social media followers and connections; your strategic partners who may want to promote your product as affiliates, in exchange for a commission on sales; and your budget for paid traffic, such as social media ads. You'll need at least one of these traffic sources to make your offer.

Finally, fully understand the value your product provides, and more importantly, be able to articulate that value to your potential customers so you can convince them to take action and purchase. The best way to do this is to know and address the pain points frustrating your potential customers. You'll need to show them how your offer can alleviate that pain.

Once you've thought about those things, create an irresistible offer with the following steps:
1. Create urgency and scarcity.
2. Use the customer's language.
3. Overcome objections.
4. Focus on benefits instead of features.
5. Use social proof.
6. Employ risk reversal.

Step 1: Create urgency and scarcity. To maximize the profitability of your launches, you must create urgency for your prospects (potential buyers) so they feel a need to buy now. Whether there's a limited quantity of products, limited number of spaces in your program, or your launch offer is only available for a limited time, you generate a sense of scarcity by adding limits to your offer. You can also generate a sense of scarcity by adding limited-time bonuses to your offer.

Step 2: Use the customer's language. Whenever and wherever you market and sell to your customers, use the exact words they would use to describe the problem your product will help them solve. If you've built your list of email subscribers or social media followers, you can poll your audience and ask them what challenges they experience. That way, you can record their answers to your questions and use their language as you build your product and craft your marketing messages.

Step 3: Overcome objections. Address head on any reasons your prospects may have for not buying. Defeat those objections in your copy on your sales page, in any videos or webinars you create, and in any emails you send out. Being proactive in overcoming objections, rather than avoiding them, makes selling that much easier because you answer the questions and concerns your potential customers already have in mind.

Step 4: Focus on benefits instead of features. Too often, entrepreneurs get caught up in sharing the features of their product because they're so excited about what they've created. But customers don't buy features. They buy what those features will do for them. A feature is an element of your product. A benefit is something your product will do for the customer. When you shop for shampoo, you want to know more than how much shampoo is in the bottle (a feature). You want to know if it will hydrate your hair, protect your hair from damage, or preserve your new hair color. Those are all benefits, and benefits are why people buy. You can share the benefits of your product by highlighting the transformation your product can provide for your customers.

Step 5: Use social proof. This is evidence that other customers, people just like your audience, have benefited from using the product. If you've never launched the product before, it may be evidence that customers have benefited from working with you or your business. You can provide social proof through testimonials, reviews, case studies, screenshots of social media posts, or statistics relevant to the people you've served. You can also attach yourself to larger brands to show you're the expert by sharing media outlets where you or your business have appeared or identify prestigious clients you've served. When you see "Our Clients Include" or "As Seen In" on marketing materials, the company is providing social proof by attaching itself to recognizable brands.

Step 6: Employ risk reversal. Customers who are hesitant to buy can often be persuaded to purchase when you take away any perceived risks that they'll lose money or regret the purchase for some other reason. Money-back guarantees are a great way to do this. Other risk-reversal strategies include free trials, name your own price, and a freemium model that allows customers to try one version of a digital product for free and upgrade to a paid version if and when they choose to do so. The right risk-reversal strategy for your launch will depend on your product, which strategy will most appeal to your audience, and how much risk you're willing and able to take on to convince customers to buy.

Too often, entrepreneurs dive into the busy work of a launch, like creating graphics and building sales pages, without taking time to plan out a great offer. When your product is priced right for your audience and you spend time ensuring each of these elements of an irresistible offer are in place, your chances of getting more sales increase greatly. To learn more about how to create an irresistible offer, check out: *Traffic, Sales & Profit: The Ultimate Step-by-Step Guide to Creating Consistent Business Revenue Online* at freetspbook.com.

Data and Budget

Data is essential to having one profitable launch and even more so to making sure your subsequent launches grow in profitability. Capturing data during your launch will allow you to optimize your launch process. During your planning process, it's imperative for you to spend some time determining what launch metrics are important for you and then put measures in place to capture those metrics.

Here are some examples of important launch metrics along with basic explanations of what they measure:

- Opt-in rate: percentage of people who see your opt-in offer and choose to subscribe to your email list in exchange for your lead magnet
- Email delivery rate: percentage of sent emails that arrive to subscribers' inboxes rather than bouncing
- Email open rate: percentage of email subscribers who open any given email you send
- Email click-through rate: percentage of email openers who click a link in the email
- Video views: number of people who viewed your video for a predetermined minimum number of seconds or minutes
- Cart conversion rate (sales): percentage of orders completed of the orders started
- Abandoned cart rate: percentage of people who click to buy your product but, for whatever reason, don't complete the order

You should also keep track of any tech glitches. If your opt-in process, email process, or sales process failed at any point, make note of what went wrong. Do everything possible to ensure it doesn't happen again in your next launch.

As you're capturing metrics during your launch, you'll be able to see where any of the metrics are falling short, and you can pivot. If your email open rate is low, you might want to change some of the subject lines. If you aren't getting enough opt-ins, you may decide to do more live videos on Facebook or Instagram. Wherever your launch isn't working the way you want, you'll know while you're in the process of launching, so you can do some things differently and increase your chances of having a more successful launch. Data is crucial to a profitable launch and to building a profitable business.

When you launch your product for the first time, you have no data to refer to from previous launches, so coming up with a budget will take research and a bit of estimating. Start with how much you want to and can invest in your launch. Depending on the professional you work with, a service like copywriting or sales page design might cost $500 or $5000. Your budget will dictate which of those vendors you can work with. Your total budget will also determine how much of the launch you'll outsource and how much you'll do yourself. If you have a $10,000 budget, and you plan to spend $3000 on marketing, then you have $7000 left to spend. That number will help you make some decisions as you plan. Tracking your expenses will also provide critical data during the launch phase so you can determine exactly how profitable your launch was.

Creating a budget for your launch involves estimating the costs of all your launch activities and aggregating those estimated costs into a document where you can compare estimated costs to the actual costs of your launch activities. No fancy software is required for budgeting. I typically create my budgets in a simple spreadsheet. To create your launch budget, start by listing all the launch activities you've identified during your launch planning. Next to that list, create a column for estimated costs, and then add a column for actual costs.

Depending on what tasks you're outsourcing, you may need cost estimates for the following launch activities:

1. Launch planning and management
2. Copywriting
3. Building sales pages
4. Planning, writing, and executing a social media marketing plan
5. Planning, writing, and executing an email marketing plan
6. Shooting and editing photos
7. Shooting and editing video content
8. Creating graphics for marketing
9. Paid advertising for marketing, including the costs of hiring an ad agency and the costs of the ads

10. Fulfillment costs, including shipping materials, postage, and shipping team members
11. Costs of the goods sold
12. Any activity unique to your launch

Once you identify all your major launch activities, you can estimate the costs associated with completing those activities. Cost estimates can be obtained by using the actual costs from similar launches, or you can consult the resources or team members who will actually complete the activities. Request an estimate for the work that needs to be completed.

As I mentioned, it's always good to start with a general idea of how much money you're planning to spend on the project. This can help you identify the right team members to work on your project based on their proposals and costs estimates. Your cost estimates can get very granular and precise. When I worked in corporate, we estimated all costs down to every hour, or even half hour, that resources worked on the project. To be honest, for my own launches, I don't include the costs for any of my efforts managing the project and executing project tasks or the costs of my internal employees' work. I do, however, include the costs of all external vendors who I hire for the project. And of course, I include the costs for paid marketing, goods sold, and fulfillment.

Once you've completed the estimating process, you can establish a baseline for all your launch costs. As you complete the activities, be sure to document the actual costs of each activity. At the end of your project, you can compare your actual costs to the estimated costs to determine how well your team performed. You can also use the actual costs to determine how profitable your launch was. And finally, you'll be able to use the actual costs as a basis for future project budgets.

It's important to make sure you have these four pillars of a profitable launch in place before you try to launch. Skipping even one of these can hinder your ability to launch or cause you to have disappointing launch results. When you have a list, an irresistible offer, the right technology, defined metrics for the data you want to capture, and a budget, you set yourself to create a profitable launch.

Profitable Launch Blueprint
Case Study | CurlMix

Kim and Tim Lewis, founders of CurlMix.com have harnessed the power of planning to take advantage of the biggest sales season of the year, Black Friday. In 2019, the Lewises 4Xed sales of their natural hair care products over their 2018 Black Friday sales numbers.

Their results included:

Total Sales	↑ $337,000
Conversion rate	4% (same as 2018)
Average order value	↑ $17
Total orders	↑ 3700
Customer return rate	↑ 20%

CurlMix's 2018 launch wasn't bad at all. Many entrepreneurs would love to bring in more than one thousand orders and almost $100,000 in sales over the course of a week. But by any measurement, their 2019 launch far outpaced 2018. They made those improvements by employing all the essential elements and strategies of a profitable launch.

Kim and Tim had all the pillars of a profitable launch in place before they started their 2019 Black Friday launch. They had a list, and they continued to build it with a small paid marketing campaign. They crafted an irresistible offer, including bonus gifts with purchase, with their customers in mind. They had technology in place from previous launches, and they had data from those launches and from testing their offer to help set their budget and expectations for the 2019 launch.

Kim says if you wait until September or October to plan your Black Friday promotions, you're already too late. She and Tim started planning in August. They planned to have the necessary inventory. They scheduled photo shoots to take place at least two months prior to their launch date. Knowing that it could take much longer than usual during the busy holiday season, they also left plenty of time to get their Facebook ads approved. In the prep phase, they took action on their plan by creating promotional materials and setting up and testing technology.

In the promotion phase, they gave away free products over the course of a week to keep the buzz high. The items were low-cost for CurlMix but provided value for customers. They launched early, starting on the Monday before Black Friday, and their promotions spanned over eight days. Everything they did on social media or through email led directly to their launch. During the promotions phase and once the cart opened for their offer, they monitored conversion rates, email open and click-through rates, and SMS response rates and made changes when necessary.

Going forward, the Lewises can analyze the data and extract and apply valuable lessons to future launches. By following a system, they've created a launch process for CurlMix, which they can use to produce more and more profits.

Visit profitablelaunchblueprint.com/resources to download free tools and templates to support your next profitable launch.

CHAPTER FOUR

The Profitable Launch Blueprint

The Profitable Launch Blueprint is the exact system I use to create successful launches in our two businesses. It's the process I teach to new entrepreneurs to help their first launch go smoothly and result in more profits. I also teach this process to seasoned entrepreneurs so they can maximize their profits and meet higher launch goals.

Remember the Profitable Launch Blueprint consists of five steps:

In this chapter, we'll break them down one by one so you know exactly what's required to implement each step for your launch.

Step One: Plan

Planning is the very first step in the Profitable Launch Blueprint because the other four steps are all likely to fall apart if they're not properly planned. Planning is the step that makes effective prep, promotions, launching, and wrap-up possible. As a former project manager, I'll confess I have a strong bias for planning. Any time I take on an important project, I start by creating a solid plan. Planning is my love language, but you don't have to be a certified project manager or love planning to make it work for you and your launch. Just follow the Profitable Launch Blueprint.

If you increase the amount of smart planning you do in your business, you will be more profitable. That's the bottom line. Investing the necessary time to adequately plan will help you address most of the challenges that come up in launches. It will separate you from the entrepreneurs who mistakenly believe they can make it up as they go along and still have a successful launch. In my work with entrepreneurs over the last several years, and in my own business, I've seen and can relate to many of these launch challenges.

The most common launch challenges include the following:
- Not selling enough
- Too few eyes on the offer
- Technology glitches
- Lack of time
- Feeling rushed and overwhelmed
- Frustration with your team or your vendors
- Launch delayed by weeks or months
- Failure to launch at all
- Some combination of the above

A project plan details the what, who, how, and when of your project. It defines what needs to be done, who will do each task, how long each task will take, when each task will happen, and how much it will cost. When your plan covers all those elements, you can effectively minimize most of those challenges and increase your chances of success. Assuming you've laid a foundation with the four pillars of a profitable launch, the very next thing you'll do is start to document your plan. (In Chapter Four, I'll walk you, step by step, through the process to create your launch plan.)

A good plan breaks a large project into small, manageable chunks and ensures no important element of the plan is overlooked. Often, entrepreneurs fail to launch their products because they're overwhelmed or afraid, but when you sit down and plan on paper, it becomes a lot easier to execute your launch. When you have a clear plan, launching doesn't seem so daunting. All you have to do is complete the next task or make sure whoever is responsible for that task gets it done on time.

Planning increases your commitment to the project. If a goal without a plan is just a wish, then a project without a plan is just a hope. A plan allows you to put measurable numbers around your launch project, create specific goals, and set your intentions to achieve those goals. Planning helps you identify potential problems and put actions in place to proactively address those problems. You can also better predict your return on investment because planning requires you to think through how much your launch will cost, how much you can spend on marketing, how much money you'll invest in ads, and any number of factors that can impact your profit margin.

To understand how much time really need for your launch, you must have a plan. Fortunately, planning also helps you make the most of your time. You'll have enough time to set up and test your technology and do more promotions. When you plan properly, you'll send more promotional emails, do more social media posts, and do more marketing overall because you won't feel too rushed to do it. Many entrepreneurs try to create promotions as they go through the promotions phase, but they underestimate how long it will take to write copy, create graphics, and test links, and their promotions suffer.

When you have a plan, working with your in-house team and with vendors becomes much easier because you can confidently convey your objectives and deadlines for your launch. Failure to provide your team with specific dates or clear expectations leads to frustration because your team, including vendors, may be working on a totally different timeline with different objectives if they don't have a clear plan to follow. This can be easily avoided with proper planning and communication of the plan.

Just as importantly, planning allows you to pivot. When you're making things up as you go along, you don't have the bandwidth to assess the performance of your launch and make changes on the fly as needed. Entrepreneurs who launch without a solid plan are typically so busy thinking about getting out promotional content that they can't focus on how the launch is performing. Looking at the data, so you can pivot and make adjustments during your launch, could make your launch more profitable, but you need time to do that analysis.

At Traffic Sales & Profit, we've seen firsthand the value of pivoting. During one special promotion, our launch ran for six days, and we monitored our metrics as we went along. We kicked off the launch with a webinar and then sent follow-up emails, but we quickly observed lower sales than we'd expected. With a quick analysis of the numbers, we realized not enough people had joined our initial webinar, so based on our typical conversion rates, we weren't on track to hit our goals.

In that case, the data told us we needed to pivot. We chose to host an additional webinar and send out more emails to encourage people to show up for it. We also changed some of the email subject lines in an effort to increase our open rates (the percentage of subscribers who opened the emails.) Finally, we increased the emails we sent after the webinar so more people would see our offer. Because we had thoroughly planned our launch, we were able to make necessary changes along the way and get back to our usual conversion rates.

When entrepreneurs fail to plan effectively, they typically spend most of their launch period focused on creating marketing and getting it out. They don't have times to look at the metrics, so they have no idea how well or how poorly the launch may be going. Even if they take a minute to look at the data, they don't have the bandwidth to optimize aspects of the launch to make it more profitable. A launch isn't something you can set on autopilot while you do other things. To get the best results, someone has to be present and available to make changes as needed. A solid plan frees you up to pay attention to how the launch is going and respond accordingly.

When I speak, teach, or coach about launching, entrepreneurs often ask me how much planning they should do. Project management industry standard suggest five to ten percent of your total project time should be spent planning. If you take a month to prepare for and execute your launch—including time spent writing emails, creating graphics, planning ads, and setting up technology—but you only spend a couple of hours jotting down your plan, that's just not enough. Ten percent of one month, excluding weekends, is two days. If you want to have a huge launch, and you know the total effort will take you more than three months, then you definitely want to spend at least a couple of weeks planning for that launch.

Problems created by a lack of planning can cost you significantly. Because of your lack of planning, you may miscalculate the total cost of your launch. You may underestimate how much you need to spend on marketing. You may miss your delivery dates for important tasks, not engage your vendors early enough, or completely miss your launch date because you couldn't manage to pull everything together in time. All these problems can be minimized or avoided with planning.

Every project, no matter how big or small, requires some level of planning. Launching is no different. If your launch will only take a couple of days to complete, then sit down for an hour or two to plan it out. As you increase the amount of time you spend planning, you're almost guaranteed to have more profitable launches. There's no way around it. Planning is essential to a profitable launch.

During the planning phase, you'll define the project and your offer, create the project schedule, engage resources, and set up collaboration tools. Depending on the complexity of your launch, it could take several weeks to define the project and create the project schedule. This process is iterative; you'll repeat some of the steps of planning, refining the plan each time.

Start your launch by hosting a project kickoff call. A typical launch could have one to three (or more) project kickoff calls. The final kickoff call will include a review of the project objectives and timelines, and all key project team members should be in attendance. (See Chapter Five for details of how to conduct kickoff calls.)

A great place to keep all the details discussed when you are defining the project is the project charter. The project charter, usually a digital file or app, serves as a hub for all important project information and assets and should be shared with every member of the project team. (See Chapter Five for more information about how to create your project charter.)

> ## GET TO WORK
>
> Below is a checklist of points to cover as you start the planning process.
> - Launch objectives
> - Core offer
> - Stack value/bonuses
> - Upsell/downsell
> - Price
> - Launch strategy
> - Launch date
> - Launch team and roles
> - Resources to engage (Contact team members/vendors to share initial launch objectives and dates and get commitments to work on the launch.)
> - Tools, systems, and other technology
> - High-level schedule (See Chapter Five.)
> - Project charter (See Chapter Five.)

Step 2: Prep

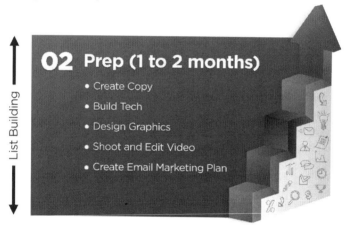

Depending on how complex your tasks are, your prep period could last up to one or two months. Sometimes it lasts two months because you don't have the budget for a team and have to complete a lot of these tasks yourself. For example, week one, you write copy. Week two, you build the landing pages. Week three, you outsource the graphics and work with a designer to get them created. Weeks four and five, you may still be building out landing pages, email marketing campaigns, and social media marketing content. It could take you a good eight weeks or more if you're doing most of these things yourself, but if you have several team members, many of these tasks can be done in parallel.

During this step, you'll build out the infrastructure of your launch, which may include the following:

- Writing copy for landing pages
- Building landing pages (opt-in pages, sales pages, order forms)
- Creating a social media plan
- Writing social posts
- Writing email copy
- Uploading emails to your email service provider
- Shooting and editing photos
- Shooting and editing videos
- Creating graphics
- Writing and designing presentations for webinars

Remember this isn't a planning stage. This is a doing stage. For example, don't just create a plan for posting on various platforms. This is the time to prepare for your launch. Actually write the posts and create graphics and videos for your social media posts. All the content you'll need for your promotional period and your launch period should be created during this prep phase.

The technology you'll use for your launch should also be purchased, if you don't already have it, and set up during this time. Your launch may require any of the following tools: collaboration tools, landing pages, email marketing software, e-commerce tools, online meeting apps, or membership platforms. Make sure you understand what tools you already have and what tools you'll need. That way, you can purchase software you need without duplicating what you already have.

> Visit profitablelaunchblueprint.com/resources for a list of technology we use for our launches.

Don't underestimate the duration or effort required to complete the activities in this phase. If you invest the necessary time in prep, you'll find it much easier to complete the next very important step for your launch: promotions.

GET TO WORK

In the prep phase, identify the resources who will complete the following activities:
- Write copy for landing pages.
- Build landing pages (opt-in pages, sales pages, order forms).
- Create social media plan.
- Write social posts.
- Create email marketing plan.

- Write email copy.
- Upload emails to email service provider.
- Shoot and edit photos.
- Shoot and edit videos.
- Create graphics.
- Write copy for webinars.
- Design presentation deck for webinars.
- Other _____
- Choose the tools you'll use for your launch and decide how you plan to use them.
- Project management: Trello, Basecamp, Teamwork, Asana
- Collaboration and project charter: Google Suite (Docs, Sheets, Chat, Drive)
- Landing pages: ClickFunnels, Leadpages
- Email marketing/SMS/CRM: Infusionsoft/Keap, ActiveCampaign, Klaviyo,
- Integrations: Zapier
- E-commerce: Shopify, Stripe
- Online meeting platform: Zoom, Skype, GoToMeeting
- Membership platform: Click Funnels, Teachable, Memberium
- Other

Step 3: Promote

Step three of the Profitable Launch Blueprint is to promote the launch. Depending on what you're launching, this period could last two weeks or more. During this time, you'll tell the world about your launch with email marketing, paid advertising, social media posts and videos, podcast appearances, or whatever combination of methods you choose to use to get the attention of the people who want what you have to offer.

Donnie Bryant, professional copywriter and marketing strategist at Donnie-Bryant.com, believes most entrepreneurs don't promote their products or services nearly enough. "They don't want to be perceived as harassing anybody. They don't want to be spammy," says Donnie. He recommends entrepreneurs promote every day, especially during a launch period. "You're not just selling. You're educating, entertaining, and inspiring people," he says. "When you give people hope that they can get the results they want, they want to hear from you."

I can't emphasize enough how often entrepreneurs fail to execute sufficient promotions for their launches and how much it costs them in potential profits. It doesn't matter if you're just starting a side business or you've already made seven figures with your product, you can probably benefit by promoting your launches more than you do right now. You can only sell your product if enough of the right people know about it and know why they should buy it. Don't ever shy away from promotions.

When you give yourself an adequate amount of time to plan (in step 1) and create (in step 2) your launch promotions, you also give yourself the opportunity to be more creative and innovative and to reach more people. With sufficient time and planning, you can come up with more ways to create buzz around your product. That could include producing more videos and crafting more and different kinds of emails, such as testimonials, unboxings, and reveals.

There are so many ways to launch and promote your product, but if you don't give yourself an adequate amount of time to plan, you can only manage to accomplish a fraction of those things. When you have plenty of time to plan and create your launch promotions, you can promote for longer periods of time. When it's appropriate for your audience and your product, you can build buzz and take your audience on a journey, over several weeks or months, leading up to your actual launch date. But you have to plan that well in advance and prepare for it.

Another benefit of planning and preparing, is that you can make the most out of your paid advertising during this promotions stage. You can start running paid ads earlier to get potential customers to sign up to your email list, register for your master class, or otherwise engage with you and give you permission to market to them. You can take time to test ads and offers to determine which are most successful before you kick off your full launch and then optimize and scale those ads during your launch period.

We've found paid ads are essential to promotions. In general, your paid advertising budget should equal ten to thirty percent of the revenue you expect to make from your launch. If your goal is to make $50,000 in revenue from your launch, budget $5000 to $15,000 for paid ads. If this doesn't fit what you've heard other experts say they invest in ads, keep in mind that many of those experts have already developed a loyal following of customers or have significant affiliate relationships with influencers they can enlist to promote their products. It's tempting to try to imitate what you see the gurus doing, but you only see a small part of the picture. You don't see the planning, the money, or the time successful entrepreneurs pour into promoting their six-figure and seven-figure launches. Launching at that level requires an investment.

Many entrepreneurs miss out on the boost paid ads can provide to their promotions. They invest little or nothing in paid advertising because they're afraid to spend the money, don't have the budget they'd like to invest, or have bought into the myth of building a seven-figure business with nothing but a laptop and the sweat of their brow. If you're expecting to bring in $100,000 with your launch, are you willing to put $10,000, $20,000, or $30,000 toward your paid advertising for that launch? If you hope to have a million-dollar launch, how much are you willing and able to invest to get there? Consider your budget and set your expectations accordingly.

While planning your promotions (in step 1 of this five-step planning process), it's important to identify which promotions strategies you'll use. Consider the type of product you're offering, whether most of your audience is cold or warm, and your price point. A higher price or a colder audience will likely require you to do more promotions. Choosing your promotions strategies will also help you set the length of your promotional period from one day to two weeks and up to one month.

Regardless of how great their products are, most entrepreneurs simply don't promote their launches enough with paid ads or otherwise. They don't put enough time, thought, effort, or money behind their launches. They don't invest their time and creativity into coming up with new ways to promote their product. Choose to handle your launch differently. Choose to invest in promotions.

Your options for promotions include, but aren't limited to the following:

- email marketing
- SMS marketing
- live or recorded webinars
- social media posts
- live social media videos
- recorded video series
- paid ads
- coordinated podcast appearances
- live events
- brand ambassadors or a launch team
- affiliates (borrowing influencers' audiences in exchange for a commission on sales)

If you start early enough, "coming soon" messaging can work with any of the above strategies and can prove incredibly effective in building buzz and a demand for your product. Done right, it will have your audience waiting with their credit cards in hand to purchase when you open cart. However, you need extra lead time to announce that you have something great in the works and make this messaging work for you.

For coming soon strategies, we've seen clients take customers on a journey with them as they develop their products. They share and ask for feedback on designs, request input on features, and share completed assets, like labels, book covers, or logo designs. They write blog posts or share video content or training related to the product they're about to launch, all in an effort to drum up excitement about their upcoming offer.

If you're using a live event, master class, webinar, or video series to promote your product, your early promotions should push people to register. Your emails, live broadcasts on Facebook or Instagram, and graphics should all lead your audience to sign up for your upcoming event. Once they register, you'll have their contact information (typically, name and email address and/or phone number to text), so you can communicate further with them about your product launch. You can also retarget the same people with engagement ads and emails to keep them interested and increase the likelihood they'll show up for the online or in-person event.

Once they've registered, reach them with engagement promotions. Everything you send out or post is designed to keep people interested and engaged so they'll actually attend the event for which they signed up. These promotions are designed to get people into your real or virtual room so you can share information with them, give value, and sell your product.

Consider the following questions while planning your promotions in the planning stage (step 1):
1. How many days, weeks, or months will I promote my launch?
2. What platforms will I use to promote my launch?
3. Will I use paid ads? If so, how much will I invest?
4. How will I use email?
5. Will I livestream on social, and/or use social posts? If so, on what social media platforms?
6. Will I host a live webinar or master class?
7. Will I record a video series?
8. Will I host a live challenge?

If you're using paid ads, put considerable planning and preparation into that process. Decide on the platforms, when those ads will run, and what call to action they'll have. Get clear on your target audience and how you'll use retargeting to get your ads in front of people more than once to increase the likelihood they'll take the action you want them to take. If your launch window is small, like four to six days, you may want to start your paid ads earlier so you can optimize and scale them during your actual launch period. Successfully running ads requires a specific set of skills, and I recommend working with a professional to make the most of your investment.

> **GET TO WORK**
>
> Consider the following when planning your promotional activities.
> - Run prelaunch promotions.
>   - How many days/weeks/months will you promote your launch?
>   - What platforms will you use to promote (i.e. – email, live videos on social, social media posts…)
> - Run launch promotions.
>   - How many open cart emails will you send?
> - Run paid ads
>   - What platforms will you use for paid ads?
>   - When will the paid ads begin?
> - Post to social media.
> - Build tech (additional launch assets).

Step 4: Launch

It's showtime! Step four of the Profitable Launch Blueprint is to finally kick off and complete your launch. Regardless of the launch method you choose, the following activities should be included in your launch.

1. Open cart.
2. Send open-cart emails.
3. Continue to promote via webinars, challenges, social media videos, or other methods.
4. Close cart.

Your open cart period is the time during which your product is available to be purchased. Keeping your cart open for a finite number of days creates scarcity and urgency for your potential customers to buy your product. During this time, continue to communicate with potential customers, especially those who have subscribed to your email list.

Let's look at an example of how you might continue to promote your product during the launch period. If you have your cart open for six days, on day one, you can send out two emails. The first email might say something like: "Hey, my cart is open, and you can purchase this amazing offer now!" Then, you can send out the second email on day one to share how sales are rolling in, welcome new customers and invite more, or apologize for any tech hiccups that might have occurred. In these emails, focus on benefits, not features, and on building excitement and buzz.

On days two through four, while your cart is open, send out one email each day. This might include an FAQ email, in which you answer the frequently asked questions about your product or lead subscribers to an FAQ video. Or you can send an email sharing testimonials or case studies from satisfied customers. You can send an email to share an unboxing of your product. You can stack the bonuses and send out an email each day to add a new bonus. And you can share more valuable content with your potential customers to push them to purchase your offer.

Then day five arrives, the day before your cart closes. On this day, send one email to remind your email subscribers they only have twenty-four hours before the cart closes and your offer disappears. Later the same day, you can send out another email with more content.

On day six, send three emails. This is the final day, and the cart is closing. Many people will have waited until the last minute to buy, so you want to remind them this is their last chance. In the morning, email your subscribers to remind them the sale ends tonight. Later, send a second email to share some relevant content or feedback from customers who have already bought. And then later that evening, around about nine o'clock your time, send one last reminder that the cart closes at midnight. Following this email schedule, you can send nine to ten emails during a six-day open-cart period. I've seen marketers send as many as twenty-five emails during this open cart period. (Often, their email lists are segmented, and they send different email content to the different segments of their lists.)

Again, most entrepreneurs don't promote their launches enough—either because they're overwhelmed, due to lack of planning, or they're afraid to bother their subscribers. You don't have to repeat their mistakes, but you'll never be able to effectively implement your email if you're drafting emails ad hoc during your launch. Even if you get them out at the last minute, they won't be as good as they could be with some planning and preparation. If you invest the time to plan out all the emails you're going to send (during step 1) and then write them (during step 2) before your launch begins, you'll be in a much better place.

Once the launch has begun, you can still edit the emails as needed, such as when you want to share additional testimonials and feedback from people who've purchased during the open-cart period, but you won't be scrambling to write them from scratch. You can also watch the performance of your launch and pivot by adding emails, switching up the content, or rewriting subject lines or email content as needed.

Once you announce a time for your cart to close, stay true to your word and close the cart at that time. It can be tempting to leave it open a little longer if you're selling well up to the last minute or if your product isn't selling well and you're feeling desperate for more sales, but don't make that mistake. If you do, you'll create a sense of distrust with your subscribers and followers. In the future, they may not buy from you because they'll see you as lacking integrity. You'll also have a hard time creating a sense of urgency because they'll expect you to break your word and leave your cart open longer than promised every time you launch a product.

However, once your cart closes, you still have an opportunity to sell to people who didn't purchase by offering them a different product of lower, higher, or equal value. Plan and write the emails, sales pages, and other copy for those additional offers in advance. Otherwise, you'll probably be too exhausted to come up with a follow-up sequence. That's the beauty of using this system. It prepares for your launch, start to finish, well in advance, so you have the time and energy to make the most of launching.

GET TO WORK

Answer the following questions as you plan your launch.
1. What type of launch is this (product launch, webinar, live event, challenge, etc.)?
2. Is this a launch with email marketing?
3. Exactly how will I launch?
4. How long will the cart remain open?
5. Will I have a sales page, an order form, or both options?
6. What type of technology will be used?
7. How many open-cart and follow-up emails will I send?

Use the following six-day launch schedule as a guide for planning your launch activities.

Day 1: 2 emails
- Cart is open
- Lots of sales rolling in / "Sorry for the glitch

Days 2 to 4: 1 email each day
- FAQs
- Webinars
- Testimonials or case study
- Unboxing
- Stack bonuses
- More content

Day 5: 2 emails
- Cart closes in 24 hours
- More content

Day 6: 3 emails
- Cart closes tonight/Sales end tonight
- Content/story
- Cart closes in 3 hours

Step 5: Wrap-up

The final step in your launch process is wrapping up, which could last one to two weeks. During this time, you'll capture metrics, document lessons learned, organize assets, and complete fulfillment activities. To capture useful metrics, include any data that can help you measure the success of your launch and improve future launches. This may include page views or visitors, page conversions, number of opt-ins, number of registrants, number of attendees, email open rates, video views, number of units sold, and profit. The goals you set and strategies you use for your launch will define what metrics you should record.

To document the lessons learned from your launch, pull your team together, within a day or two after your cart closes, and discuss what went well, what went wrong, and what needs to be focused on during the next launch. Document all these observations in detail. Also, make sure your assets are organized. Remember your project charter is the hub for all your launch assets and provides a place for your team to access what they need. (See Chapter Five for more information on the project charter.) Graphics, images, emails, copy, videos, a list of vendors you used, and your updated project plans should all be filed in folders in your project charter so they can be used for your next launch.

Your fulfillment activities may include granting access to online portals, shipping physical products, shipping or emailing bonuses, and onboarding clients to your programs. Many entrepreneurs are exhausted at the end of their launches, and they're really tempted to take a break and delay this important step. However, it's important to follow through on all fulfillment activities right away. Otherwise, you'll end up with high return rates, disgruntled customers, and negative word of mouth that can damage your business reputation and hurt your next launch. If you plan accordingly, a lot of your fulfillment can be automated, but making sure it happens and quickly resolving any issues should still be part of your wrap-up plan.

Many entrepreneurs are so worn out—and either so relieved or disappointed—after launching that they drop the ball on the wrap-up. However, if you take the time to look at your metrics, organize your assets, look at your lessons learned, and ensure successful fulfillment, you're much more likely to have an even more successful launch next time. Your launch isn't over until you complete this last step. No matter how small, how large, or how quick your launch is, it should include all five steps of the Profitable Launch Blueprint.

> **GET TO WORK**
>
> Consider the following when planning your wrap-up activities.
> - Determine how to capture metrics.
> - Schedule a meeting to discuss and document lessons learned.
> - Create online folders to organize assets.
> - Identify fulfillment activities.

> Visit profitablelaunchblueprint.com/resources to download free tools and templates to support your next profitable launch.

PROFITABLE LAUNCH CASE STUDY | DUNAMIS WOMAN ENTERPRISE

Ariel Fuller and Pastor Davetta "Dee" Collins are the founders Dunamis Woman Enterprise. The mission of their company is to guide women of faith to transform their life and relationships. When this dynamic mother-daughter duo ran a free seven-day challenge called "Sexual Healing for the Woman in You," they used paid Facebook ads to promote the challenge to people in their target demographic and push them to join. They also promoted the challenge to their email list, and then they hosted the challenge in their private Facebook group, going live every day to teach their group members. During this faith-based challenge, they shared prayers and scriptures as well as motivational training. They challenged the women to take action because they wanted participants to experience a real transformation. At the end of the seven-day sales challenge, they held webinars and live events to launch their paid program.

Challenges are a great way to build your list and your audience and to re-engage and re-energize the people who've been on your list for a while. With their challenge, Ariel and Dee grew their email list by 65 percent. They went from 5,900 subscribers on their email list to 9,735 subscribers. They didn't create a new group for this challenge, so their existing Facebook group grew by 123%. Before the challenge, the group consisted of 2,863 members, and after the challenge, they had 6,318 members. Ariel and Dee generated a total launch revenue of $13,690, an almost a 297% increase over the revenue generated from their previous challenge.

When they attended our TSP Live Conference, Ariel and Dee learned new information and received input on how to run a successful challenge. One of our speakers presented on the topic, and Ariel and Dee asked for suggestions from the TSP community, particularly their fellow members of the TSP mastermind group. In addition, they took advantage of the challenge master class available in the mastermind group resources. Ariel and Dee applied what they learned, so they didn't have to reinvent the wheel. They used templates and proven steps from people who have conducted successful challenges to create a successful challenge of their own.

Let's look at the Profitable Launch Blueprint as they applied it. They used the challenge to grow and re-engage their email list. As a part of the challenge, they livestreamed in their Facebook group, emailed their list, sent out surveys to gather data, created lead magnets, and provided content. They also promoted their seven-week challenge for several weeks before the challenge began, which required a lot of planning.

The main difference between this launch and their previous launch was the planning. Although the first launch was great, the transformation the women received from their last challenge didn't quite match up with the offer at the end, so their offer didn't convert well. They didn't have many sales the first time around, but this time, they really thought all that out during the planning stage. They focused on their brand story and the journey they were taking these women on. That journey led them to the offer they presented at the end. They also planned and scheduled their social media posts and were able to do more social media posting because of it. They made sure that all hands were on deck for planning and executing the plan well.

Ariel and Dee invested a lot of time in designing their offer and focused on improving their use of technology each and every time they launched. While they utilized existing landing pages, they improved upon them in many ways. They also implemented chat bots for the first time to provide automated responses to potential customers. Messaging with the chat bot helped increase audience engagement in their launch. Instead of hiring a production company, they created original gifs and videos to further increase engagement.

They quadrupled their ad spend over what they'd spent for previous challenges, and they did this without cutting into profits because sales of their $4.95 ebook covered the cost of ads. Prior to the start of the challenge, they gave away online courses, t-shirts, and books, to keep people engaged and excited about the challenge beginning. This was especially effective because the giveaways promoted the challenge for several weeks before it began.

Data is Ariel's love language, and she collected a lot of data for this launch. Prior to planning their launch, they surveyed their email subscribers to ask about their biggest struggles. They used that information to formulate the topic for the challenge and to create the offer. After the challenge, they surveyed challenge participants. This time, they wanted to know how the audience heard about the challenge, where they were in their relationships before the challenge, how their relationships had changed since the challenge, what they liked about the Facebook group, and what other challenges they'd like to participate in with the group. This data will help them plan marketing, offers, challenges, and products in the future.

Ariel and Dee also collected a lot of personal data through the challenge, such as name, email, state, reason for joining, marital status, and age. Information about location was particularly helpful because Ariel and Dee often do tours when they launch. This will help them select the cities for their tour stops.

Other data they collected included the number of challenge sign-ups, the challenge ad spend, ad clicks, ad leads, cost per lead, and revenue they collected from the lead. They tracked how much money they made from product offers, how many sign-ups they got for the master class, total video views, comments on videos, email subscribers, and Facebook group membership stats. They calculated the total product revenue, the total master class revenue, and the total launch revenue. All this data will be used when they launch again in the future.

CHAPTER FIVE

How to Build a Launch Plan

Before you get into the work of building the plan for your launch, it's important to understand exactly what a plan is. Too many entrepreneurs write a to-do list and think they have a plan. That's a set-up for a failed launch. Instead, get a good grasp of what planning entails and learn a few essential project management definitions, and you'll be way ahead of the average business owner. Applying this knowledge will increase your chances of meeting or exceeding your profit goals every time you launch.

Consider the entire effort of planning and executing your launch, from beginning to end—from planning to wrap-up—as a single project. If you intend to launch, but you haven't articulated in writing your objectives, time frame, budget, and plan of action with dates attached to each task, you don't have an official project plan. This puts your launch at risk.

Your project plan covers the what, who, how, and when of your project. It includes a list of what needs to be done, who will do each task, how long the task will take, and most importantly, when these tasks will happen. "When" requires start and completion dates for each task, a crucial element that will keep you on track to launch as scheduled. All these elements are required to have an effective plan.

Especially when they're just beginning, most entrepreneurs underestimate the amount of planning they should do for their launches. Five to ten percent of your total project time should be spent planning. If you don't know the total project time, you'll have to estimate. If you believe it will take you four months to prepare for and execute your next launch, that equals roughly seventeen weeks. In that case, allocate at least two to three weeks to focus on planning your launch. Give yourself at least three weeks to conduct an initial project kickoff call, take the input from that call to build the plan, contact people to work on the project (engage resources), and then conduct a final project kickoff call.

When I managed large, complex software development projects, initial planning could take months. At the end of the day, your planning and your effort should match your expectation for your launch. You can't expect to have a million-dollar launch when you haven't invested any time in planning, so adjust your expectations to match the time you're willing to put into planning. The more you launch, the better you'll get at predicting your total project time and calculating the time you need to plan.

Ideally, you'll conduct your yearly planning for the upcoming year in October or November of the current year. During that yearly planning, you can identify all the launches you want to do in the next twelve months and map them on the calendar. If you want to release your book in the first quarter with a huge promotional launch, look at the calendar and select a potential date for the book launch, say March 31st. Then you can back up from there to estimate how long your preparation and promotional periods would last. If it will take three months for those activities. You probably need to kick off this project and start planning for it in December, if not November.

Once you complete that exercise for one launch, you can map out other launch goals on the calendar to see how many major launches you can realistically have each year. For instance, if Black Friday is a huge revenue generator for your business, back up from there and identify that you need to start planning for Black Friday in July or August. When you take the time to plan out your year at a high-level, you can easily identify when you need to start planning for your major launches. Put those dates on your calendar to remind you that, in July, your team needs to come together and start planning for the best, most profitable Black Friday your company has ever seen.

So many business owners fall short with planning for the last step, the wrap-up, especially fulfillment. They don't adequately plan for shipping physical products, including when will they be shipped, what shipping supplies or inventory are needed, and how many team members will be needed to support fulfillment. They don't plan for the issues that can occur with onboarding members to membership groups or providing access to digital products. Service-based business owners often fail to invest time in planning out the details of onboarding new clients and delivering the service. Your launch can fall apart with bad reviews, returns, and refund requests if fulfillment isn't handled properly, so it's worth planning to do it right.

As you launch more and more, you'll accumulate real data to help you better predict how long it will take you to execute future launches, which means you can more accurately plan. In project management, we go through exhaustive planning and estimating exercises before we settle on our launch dates. In your real world as a business owner, each launch will serve as a planning and estimating exercise for you.

Kickoff Call and High-Level Schedule
Before you build your detailed plan, create a high-level schedule. This schedule will be the framework for

your detailed launch plan. To craft the schedule, have your initial project kickoff call with all your team members. During this meeting, get buy-in from your team members on objectives. Solicit their expert opinions on how long tasks will take, and confirm their availability to complete tasks within the desired time frames.

During this call, answer the following questions:
1. What's our launch objective?
2. What are we selling?
3. What's our offer?
4. What technology will we need?
5. How will we promote the offer?
6. What preparation is needed?
7. When and how will we launch?
8. How long will our launch period be?
9. What metrics will we use to determine our success?
10. How much time do we need to invest in planning for this launch?

After answering these questions, you and your team will have a big-picture understanding of your launch strategy. Once you make those decisions, you can begin to build your high-level launch schedule—scheduling time for planning, prep, promotions, launch, and wrap-up. It's important to note that you need to start with the end in mind. To build your high-level schedule, start by selecting the date that you want to launch on, the date that your cart opens for sales, and work backwards from there.

Let's say you want to launch in March, kick off sales during a free webinar on March 15th, and then keep the cart open (sell your offer) for four days after the webinar. You'll open cart on March 15th, and sell through the 19th, when your cart will close. Working your way backwards from there, you decide you need two weeks to promote the webinar. That means you'll begin promoting the free webinar on March 1st. Pencil that date in as the start of your promotional period. That's the beginning of your high-level launch schedule.

Backing up from March 1st, determine how long it will take you and your team to create the slide presentation for the webinar, write the copy for the landing page, write the email series for people who sign up for the webinar, create social media posts and graphics, and build out sales pages, "thank you" pages, and any upsells and downsells you want to offer. If this is your first time doing this kind of launch, you might schedule eight weeks to get everything ready for your launch promotions. That takes you back to the beginning of January or end of December. According to this high-level schedule, you should begin planning this launch in early December.

Since your cart closes on March 19th, you can plan your wrap-up activities to occur during the following week or two. Put those activities on the calendar roughly through the end of March. Now you have an end-to-end high-level schedule.

The next step is to use this schedule to build a more detailed plan in your project management tool. Using the five-step planning process that follows, get granular with your plan. Remember that, until you identify the tasks that need to be done, assign resources to the tasks, and estimate the effort it will take to do the work, you don't have a plan. Over the next couple of weeks, while you're planning, use this schedule to coordinate with your team.

Reach out to resources, like your Facebook ads manager, graphic designer, or copywriter, to get on their calendars and receive input from them for your launch campaign. Ask them to commit to supporting your project so they can tell you what their implementation process looks like, what the costs will be, and what assets they'll need from you to be effective. They may even want to start work a bit earlier than your schedule suggests. For instance, your Facebook ads manager may want extra time to optimize your ads and scale them to be ready for your campaign. Also, connect with a developer to build out your technology, like landing pages. Ask him or her to pencil you in now so you can be sure of their availability when it's time to do the work.

Lock in your resources early. They'll give you additional tasks for your plan, things to do to help them help you, and you can add these tasks to your project plan. As you get closer to your launch date, send them reminders of the dates you plan to use their services. Keep reminding them, and you'll have much more success with your vendors. (Tip: One sure way to lock in dates with resources is to pay them with an initial deposit for the work and sign an agreement.)

The 5-Step Process to Build a Detailed Plan

My five-step planning process will help you go from a high-level schedule to a detailed launch plan. The five steps are:
1. Define the project.
2. Break the project into tasks.
3. Create a project schedule.
4. Assign the work.
5. Track progress.

Keep cycling through steps two through four—breaking larger task into more manageable tasks, creating a schedule for them, and assigning the work to right people—until you feel you have a solid plan. Once you're done with all that, you can present the plan to your team, get started on execution, and track your progress.

Step 1. Define the project.
During your first kickoff call, start your project charter, the document that defines the objectives and scope of your project and identifies the people working on the project. Your project charter is also a repository for all your important project assets. Back in the day, project managers used a template in Microsoft Word to create a project charter. These days, I typically use a Google Doc or Google Sheet, which allows me to link out to other documents, including sub-plans, like marketing plans and social media plans.

As a business owner, so much power to determine whether your launch will be a success or failure. Step one helps you define your project, in this case your launch, and steps two through four help you build a detailed plan for your project to increase your chances of hitting your launch goals.

Step 2. Break the project into tasks.
In this step, you'll break your high-level plan into tasks and create a detailed schedule. Your plan will cover launch prep, promotions, launch, and wrap-up. If you schedule eight weeks for prep, as in our example above, spell out exactly what must be accomplished during those eight weeks to prepare for your promotions and your launch.

Let's say you need to build landing pages, write copy for emails, create a marketing plan, create and schedule social media posts, and shoot and edit videos. Break those tasks down even further. For instance, building a sales page could be comprised of several tasks, including writing the copy, creating images, integrating the page with a credit card processor and email marketing software, and testing the funnel from end to end to make sure all the links, apps, and integrations work properly. Break every big task into as many small tasks as possible. Get as granular as you can with the tasks required for prep, promotions, launch, wrap-up.

Each task will have both duration (the time over which the task is completed) and effort (the hours invested in completing task). A task that takes four hours (effort) to complete could be completed over two days (duration). For instance, it may only take you four hours of effort to write the copy for your landing page. However, because you're still running a business and you have other things to do throughout the day, you may only have two hours per day to devote to copywriting. In that case, it may take you two days to complete that task. The duration in your plan for the copywriting task would be two days, and the effort would be four hours. Break each task down to its smallest parts, so no task takes more than eight hours of effort and no more than two weeks' duration. Any task that takes longer should be broken down further.

Steps 3 and 4. Create a project schedule and assign the work.

You can't do step three without also completing step four, so I typically talk about them together. When you create the project schedule, you'll also need to get your team members to buy in on the plan. When your team has buy-in, they're more likely to give you helpful input on their assigned tasks and deliver on time and as agreed. Often, they'll also have ideas to make your launch go more smoothly, and they can give you a good estimate of how long each task under their purview will take to complete.

Work with your team members to create a detailed project schedule with start and end dates for each task. They may point out that you need to break a task down into smaller steps. Trust their expertise and adjust your plan accordingly. Once you create the schedule and assign the work, different team members can often work on their assigned areas at the same time.

After you create your plan from end to end, hold your final project kickoff meeting, and include all the key stakeholders, anyone actively involved in completing the project. If any of your vendors have major roles and are crucial to the success of your project, consider including them in this meeting too. Review the project from start to finish with the entire team and confirm all dates.

Step 5. Track your progress.

As you and your team execute the plan, review the plan frequently and make sure it's on track. For large-scale projects, meet weekly with your team to review progress. As the project nears completion, particularly in the final couple of weeks before your launch day, meet at least a couple times per week, if not every day, to make sure everyone is on track with their tasks.

Let's put this in perspective with a real-world example. When we hold a large event, like TSP Live and TSP Game Plan, we spend at least six months planning it. We initially meet once a month for the first two to three months, and we gradually increase the frequency of our meetings. About two months before the event, we start holding weekly meetings with our team. In the final month leading up to the event, we meet at least twice a week. And in the last two weeks, we meet every day. In these meetings, we discuss project status, which includes what has been completed, what's in progress, and what's coming up in the next week or two. We also address open issues and actions to complete.

Your project manager, whether that's you or someone else, should dedicate a block of time each week to review the plan, understand the progress, and update the plan. That way, when your project manager arrives at the meeting, she or he is ready to speak to the project status. Your project manager can also create and present a status report to summarize what tasks are completed or outstanding, where the project stands in relation to due dates and budget, any potential issues, and next steps.

The project manager is responsible for making sure the team is aware of upcoming tasks and keeping everyone focused on the plan and all relevant deadlines. As the project manager for your launch, you may be the only person looking at the plan in the context of the big picture, so it's up to you to frequently remind your team of your launch goals and deadlines. If you're the person responsible for the plan, check in several times a week to make sure everybody is focused on the dates. Let them know what's due this week and that you're looking forward to receiving it.

When you follow this five-step method to build your detailed launch plan, you'll have a much better chance of success because every launch, no matter how big or small, requires planning. Commit five to ten percent of your total project time to go through this five-step process and create your profitable launch plan. When you do, you'll save time and money, and you'll make the launch experience much less stressful.

Profitable Launch Case Study | Urban Intellectuals

By the time Freddie Taylor learned the strategies in the Profitable Launch Blueprint, his company was already a seven-figure enterprise. Urban Intellectuals creates and sells products that make it fun and easy to learn Black history, and their Black history flashcards filled a huge void in the marketplace. They consistently sold well, but Freddie had another line of business that still had tremendous room to grow and scale. The Sankofa Club, a membership site that provides educational resources with an emphasis on Black history for pre-kindergarten to sixth-grade students, needed his attention.

Freddie, who says he prefers to move fast, had never spent much time planning his launches for the membership site, and the rush to launch without developing a full plan was costing him sales. "I would come up with an idea in the morning, and by the afternoon, we had what we thought was a launch plan laid out," says Freddie. After discovering Traffic, Sales, & Profit, and joining our mastermind, where I teach the Profitable Launch Blueprint strategies, Freddie realized he could do a lot more to maximize his launches.

Initially, he was resistant to slowing down and making time to plan. Freddie worried any change to his workflow wouldn't be worth the effort, but he soon saw the benefit of giving himself and his team a comprehensive plan. From the very beginning, seeing each element of a launch detailed in black and white gave Freddie, who considers himself a visual learner, a way to zero in on the details that mattered. At a glance, he could pick out what was missing, what needed to be changed, and what was solid and ready to go in his launch plan.

Although Freddie felt stretched by the planning process, each time he launched, he found it less challenging and more helpful, and soon, he couldn't deny the benefits of planning properly. He was able to look at his year and plan months in advance for each launch. Each launch went more smoothly because he was able to give team members and vendors clear timelines, and the team used assets saved in the project charter from one launch to the next. Freddie says, "At first, slowing down to plan and pay attention to every detail was like torture to me, but it really has made a difference."

Over an eight-month period, Freddie employed the Profitable Launch Blueprint to grow his email subscriber list by hosting webinars that led into challenges. The first challenge brought in just over 10,000 subscribers. The second added 44,000 leads to the list, and the third added close to 72,000 leads. The Sankofa Club went from approximately $1100 monthly recurring revenue to $22,000 a month. At over $250,000 annual revenue and growing, Freddie credits his new planning skills with getting the membership site up to and into six figures. He's still an action-taker, but that action now includes robust planning for every launch. He can see a clear path to making this a seven-figure line of business and to growing Urban Intellectuals to the next level. "You can't just luck into eight figures," says Freddie. "You actually need to have a plan."

> Visit profitablelaunchblueprint.com/resources to download free tools and templates to support your next profitable launch.

CHAPTER SIX

The Quick Launch

You may be thinking the Profitable Launch Blueprint is great, but you may also be wondering if you can use it when you want to launch something quickly. The answer to this question is yes. You can use the Profitable Launch Blueprint for a quick launch, but you can only do so if you already have some things in place. You already have an established audience that knows, likes, and trusts you. You've launched before, so you have assets in place and established timelines and processes for executing your launch. If it's a quick launch of a new product, you should have existing systems you can leverage. If you want to do a quick launch of a product you've launched before you might change the dates on an existing plan or even relaunch the exact same promotion. A quick launch takes advantage of work you've already done.

Recently, I heard Jeff Walker, creator of the Product Launch Formula, share details of a quick launch he did for his program. (He called it a pivot launch.) He explained that he enrolled seven hundred people into his program and made over one million dollars. So yes, a quick launch is possible. But Jeff had several key things in place that allowed him to execute that quick launch.

Jeff has been doing business online since 1996, when we were still using dial-up service to connect to the internet. He has a huge audience, and he has launched many times before, so he has established systems, assets, and processes in place. Jeff also has an experienced team to help him execute his launches. When you look at it that way, Jeff's quick launch success was years in the making. He normally only launches that program once a year, but he spends months planning for his annual launch. Jeff is considered a launch guru, so if he spends months planning for his multi-million dollar launches every year, you should spend much more time preparing for yours.

No matter how quickly you launch, it's still necessary to take some time before you get started to really map out what you're doing. In a quick launch, the planning and the implementing will essentially occur in parallel. You can complete your plan in one to three hours, and then revisit and update the plan every day as you implement. Reusing an existing plan is the ideal strategy for a quick launch.

As for step two, prep, keep things simple for a quick launch. Minimize the technology you use, and keep the number of landing pages as low as possible to get the job done. Trying to do a quick launch when you have to create everything from scratch is a huge endeavor and usually a mistake. To launch quickly, it's imperative to have project assets you can update and reuse. Update and reuse graphics, copy, and landing pages. Reuse, reuse, reuse. Depending on how many assets you have available to reuse and how much help you have from your team, you may be able to complete this step in as little as one to five days.

The goal of the quick launch is to quickly complete the planning and preparation so you can compress your launch timeline. You don't necessarily have to do quick promotions (step 3) in your quick launch. However, if you really want to quickly get to your launch, then you may only spend a few days promoting.

Just as with your promotions, you don't necessarily have to streamline or shorten anything in step four, your launch. You can still have your cart open for four to ten days. The quick part of the quick launch is streamlining steps one, two, and three to open cart and start making sales more quickly.

Of course, once the launch is over, you can do step five, your wrap-up, at your normal pace, but remember to do all the activities you would do in your wrap-up for any launch—especially fulfillment. The Profitable Launch Blueprint is designed to support launching and relaunching at a faster pace, and wrap-up is essential to that goal. If you properly file your assets, as you should in step five, they'll be accessible for reuse. They'll be at your fingertips, so you won't have to search for them. You'll have the necessary data and lessons learned about what worked and what you should do differently in the future, and then you can relaunch much more quickly next time around.

Profitable Launch Best Practices

Over more than two decades of managing projects, I've developed several tried-and-true project management practices. Many of these I took from my corporate job and successfully applied to launches in our business. They allowed us to make our launches more profitable and eliminate a lot of the challenges and frustrations many entrepreneurs encounter when they launch a product. These best practices can help you implement the Profitable Launch Blueprint more effectively.

Best practice #1: Every plan must have a start date and end date. Many entrepreneurs take the step of writing down a list of things to do for their launch but fail to give those tasks start dates and end dates. When you put dates on your plan and on each task, you increase your commitment to getting them done. When you don't, you don't have a plan. You have another to-do list. Dates allow you to hold yourself and your team accountable.

Best practice #2: Regularly meet with your team to track progress and discuss status. Many entrepreneurs create great plans, but then, they never refer to them again. They end up missing the dates they've set for themselves, missing their goals, and losing out on potential profits. If you don't want to fall short of you goals or miss your launch date, meet with your team on a regular schedule and make sure all tasks stay on track to be completed on time.

Best practice #3: A plan is not final until you have commitment from the resources. Unless you'll be the only person executing the plan, you must meet with your team and your vendors to get clarity on the tasks involved and the effort and duration required for each task. That way, you can build a realistic plan with realistic dates. Your plan really isn't final until you have commitment, input, and buy-in from your resources.

Best practice #4: Make your plan as detailed as possible. Never try to move forward with your launch with only a high-level plan. Create a high-level plan, and then get granular. Break big tasks into smaller tasks and be as specific as possible.

Best practice #5: No task should take longer than two weeks in duration. When your tasks take a month or two to complete, you increase the chance that you won't complete the tasks or meet your dates. If you start missing deadlines, you may get to the end of a two-month period and not have enough time to finish the work. If tasks will take longer than two weeks, break them down into smaller tasks.

Best practice #6: Take responsibility for your dates. If you ask a vendor to complete a part of your project by a specific date, periodically check in to make sure they're on track. Don't assume your dates are a priority for that vendor. Your vendors have other clients, and your work may not be at the top of their list when other clients regularly call to check on progress and you don't. No matter who owns responsibility for completing a task, make sure you own responsibility for communicating and tracking progress.

Best practice #7: Make sure someone is responsible for the entire launch plan, whether that's you or a different project manager. Someone has to be responsible for the success and execution of your plan from start to finish. Someone has to take ownership. There has to be someone in charge. Most entrepreneurs will manage their own launches. If that's the case for you, take responsibility by regularly checking on progress. Never leave a conversation, whether it's verbal or written, without revisiting the dates. Send out friendly reminders with plenty of time to get the task completed, and as the deadline approaches, check in more often.

Launching your product is a project. These project management best practices will help you eliminate frustration, minimize missed deliverables and deadlines, and avoid confusion about the objective of the launch. Take them on and make them your regular habits for your next launch and beyond.

> Visit profitablelaunchblueprint.com/resources to download free tools and templates to support your next profitable launch.

CHAPTER SEVEN

Getting Started with Your Profitable Launch

Launching your product can definitely be a daunting process. Looking at the Profitable Launch Blueprint, you may feel a little overwhelmed. However, the process of planning—the very first step in the system—alleviates much of that feeling. Breaking down huge tasks into manageable chunks helps you see how and when those things can get done. Seeing your progress as you execute the plan will motivate you to keep going.

Launches get better and easier as you do more of them, learn from each experience, and apply what you learn. The first time you launch, you may feel dissatisfied with the technology your budget allows you to use, the pages you built, how much marketing you do, your email open rates, and the amount revenue and profits you bring in. But as you launch more and more, you'll learn from each experience and improve. You'll analyze, optimize, and do it better the next time.

As you read this, you may be excited to plan and execute your first launch, but don't try to rush the process. You can have a great plan, but if you don't have essential elements in place, that plan is destined to fail. Remember you must have the four pillars of a profitable launch solidly in place before you launch. You need to a list (yours or an affiliate's), an irresistible offer (which requires a product), technology, data, and a budget.

Once you have the basics squared away, create your high-level schedule. Start with the end—your launch date—in mind and work backward to get a clear overview of what your calendar will look like as your ramp up to your launch. Hold a kickoff call with your team members and get their buy-in and input. Create your project charter and build your project plan for your launch.

With your plan in place, your next step will be prep. Get all your copy, graphics, images, videos, and landing pages created. Write your emails. Set up and test your technology. Completing this work during the prep phase gives you time to be more creative and pivot when needed once you start running promotions. During promotions, pay attention to what's working and what's not and make changes based on the numbers, like opt-in rates, email open rates, click-through rates, or webinar attendance rates.

During your launch, you can also make changes based on results like sales conversion rates and abandoned cart rates. If you've done thorough planning and prep, you should have time to add more follow-up emails or change your retargeting campaigns as needed. Wrap up by completing all fulfillment activities. File your launch assets where you can easily find and repurpose them. Analyze the data, extract the lessons, and apply them to the next launch. Most importantly, make sure your customers are taken care of and receive your product or service as promised.

The Profitable Launch Blueprint doesn't require you to produce a perfect launch, but it gives you the tools to execute your launches better. Don't strive for perfection. Just follow the system and take action. Take the first step, and the next one, and the next one to create your profitable launch.

> Visit profitablelaunchblueprint.com/resources to download free tools and templates to support your next profitable launch.

The Profitable Launch Blueprint Glossary

Duration: the period over which a task in a plan will be completed

Effort: the time invested in completing a task in a plan

High-level schedule: a big-picture schedule, created by starting with the open-cart date and working backwards; provides a framework for the launch plan

Kickoff call: a call or series of calls with resources and team members and the project manager to create the high-level schedule; may include relevant vendors

Launch: the process of releasing a product or service to the marketplace

Launch project plan: documents how you will prep for, promote, execute, and wrap up your launch.

Project: a series of interrelated tasks to accomplish a clearly defined desired objective within a specified time frame; requires a budget and a plan of action

Project charter: a hub for all important project information, including objectives, resources, roles, and responsibilities, and project assets

Project manager: person responsible for planning the project—including budget and timeline—organizing and directing the completion of the project, and guiding and executing the completion of the project; owns the success or failure of the project

Project plan: documents what tasks will be done, who will do each task, how, how long each task will take, and when each task will be started and completed

ABOUT THE AUTHOR

Recognizing the need for positive images of black marriage in the media, Ronnie founded BlackandMarriedWithKids.com (BMWK) in 2007 along with husband Lamar. Over the last twelve years, she has grown the site from a personal blog shared by one couple to an international brand with over 600,000 social media fans.

Under the couple's Tyler New Media company umbrella, Ronnie has co-produced seven films that deal with the challenges and triumphs of marriage in the black community. The couple was named one of Ebony Magazine's Power 100 in 2011 and 2012.

Prior to Tyler New Media, Ronnie Tyler spent 17 years with IBM as a Certified Project Management Professional (PMP) managing projects with 30 million dollar budgets and up to 30 developers spread across 4 continents. She now uses her skills and expertise to manage 7-figure product launches and events for Tyler New Media, LLC and their various brands, mainly Traffic Sales & Profit and BlackandMarriedwithKids.com.

Ronnie believes that, by default, every entrepreneur or small business owner is a project manager at some point in their business. Therefore, she has made it her mission to share project management best practices that will not only increase efficiency but profitability in your business.

Made in the USA
Columbia, SC
09 February 2023